100

THINGS TO DO IN
SPOKANE
BEFORE YOU
DIE

Photo credit: Colin Mulvany

100

THINGS TO DO IN
SPOKANE
BEFORE YOU
DIE

THE SPOKESMAN-REVIEW STAFF

Library of Congress Control Number: 2018945694

ISBN: 9781681061825

Design by Jill Halpin

Cover Image: Dan Pelle

Printed in the United States of America
18 19 20 21 22   5 4 3 2 1

Please note that websites, phone numbers, addresses, and company names are subject to change or cancellation. We did our best to relay the most accurate information available, but due to circumstances beyond our control, please do not hold us liable for misinformation. When exploring new destinations, please do your homework before you go.

Photo credit: Kathy Plonka

CONTENTS

• •

Music and Entertainment

• •

Sports and Recreation

• •

• •

Shopping and Fashion

PREFACE

Unless you're from around here, Spokane is one of those places that almost no one pronounces correctly. It's a pretty friendly place, but people aren't nearly as likely to tell you where to get a good cup of coffee or where to find huckleberries if you can't say Coeur d'Alene or Pend Oreille the right way.

So, before you read any further, you have to promise you'll at least try to say the names of those places correctly. That's because we're about to tell you the good stuff.

You might have heard about our famous hotel, but do you know what to eat there? Yes, we have a river, complete with breathtaking falls, running through the middle of the city, but did you know you can raft right downtown?

Or that during summer we fill the streets of Spokane with basketball hoops and invite thousands of people to play in the nation's largest three-on-three competition?

Or that our most famous resident had more hit songs than Elvis, the Beatles, and Michael Jackson combined? Bing Crosby even won an Oscar. And you can see it at Gonzaga University, another local name outsiders rarely pronounce correctly.

The Spokesman-Review has been this region's daily newspaper for 135 years. We know things. And we love to share the secrets behind our amazing clock tower and the gargoyles that guard our sister newspaper's building.

• •

To help you have the best possible Spokane experience, here's a quick pronunciation guide so you can talk like a local:

- Spokane (Spo Can—with a long *o*)
- Coeur d'Alene (Core Duh Lane)
- Pend Oreille (Ponder Ray)
- Gonzaga (Gone Zag Uh)

I look forward to seeing you at the county fair. I'll be there chowing down on giant elephant ears, a local favorite. Trust me, they're delicious.

Rob Curley
Editor, *The Spokesman-Review*

ACKNOWLEDGMENTS

When our staff started brainstorming ideas for *100 Things to Do in Spokane before You Die*, everyone began talking at once about favorite places to take family and friends. There were outdoor adventures. Cool concerts. Iconic watering holes. Fine dining spots they enjoy again and again.

Sports Editor Ralph Walter stayed quiet then finally blurted out, "Burgers! We gotta tell people where to get a burger. Nothing fancy. Just a great burger!" And so No. 8 on the list is Ralph's Nostalgic Burger Tour of Spokane.

Writers, editors, and photographers throughout *The Spokesman-Review* newsroom pitched in to create this handy bucket list for locals and visitors alike. Food editor Adriana Janovich took the lead writing the Food and Drink section. Carolyn Lamberson and the features team, including Kimberly Lusk, Treva Lind, Azaria Podplesky, and Ryan Horlen, offered dining ideas, too, plus entertainment, culture, and shopping picks.

Rich Landers and Eli Francovich anchored the Sports and Recreation section, sharing highlights from the Outdoors beat, always a huge favorite with both print and online readers in the Inland Northwest.

Throughout you'll find insights and insider tips, courtesy of Jonathan Brunt, John Stucke, Rob Curley, Mary Beth Donelan,

Becky Kramer, Kip Hill, Nick Deshais, Nathanael Massey, Jim Meehan, Rachel Sun, and Shawn Vestal.

Photographers Colin Mulvany, Kathy Plonka, Dan Pelle, Jesse Tinsley, Tyler Tjomsland, and Liz Kishimoto shared favorite images. Other contributors include Lindsey Treffry, Joe Palmquist, Rick Bonino, Mike Schmeltzer, and Jim Price.

Donna Wares and Carolyn Lamberson edited the book.

The hardest part of this project? Paring down an ever-growing list for a slim volume of just 100 picks.

What bucket list destinations did we miss? Please share your favorites by messaging bookclub@spokesman.com. Or share on social media with the hashtag #100ThingsSpokane.

• •

Photo credit: Liz Kishimoto

FOOD AND DRINK

EAT BREAKFAST ON A TRAIN
AT FRANK'S DINER

Spokane loves trains. Like, really loves trains. You'll find three choices if you want to enjoy a hearty breakfast in a historic rail car. Frank's Diner has two locations, but the most popular one is downtown. The ornate presidential-car setting and Frank's wide variety of eggs Benedict dishes (six, including a spicy Creole version) are always worth a visit. Or for a cozy, neighborhood experience, try Knight's Diner, a local haunt since 1949 that offers counter-only seating for breakfast and lunch. Owner Vicki Green is a bright presence who dotes on young train lovers. She shapes their pancakes in the shape of their age. Lunch at Knight's is good, too, with homemade soups and pies. The cranberry walnut pie is a must.

Frank's Diner
Downtown: 1516 W. Second Ave., 509-747-8798
North Spokane: 10929 N. Newport Highway, 509-465-2464
franksdiners.com

Knight's Diner
2909 N. Market St., 509-484-0015
knightsdiner.com

SIP WITH A VIEW
AT ARBOR CREST

At Arbor Crest, the wines pair perfectly with the sweeping views at this cliff-top estate set amid lush gardens. Grab friends and head to the Cliff House, perched high above the Spokane Valley. You can pack a picnic, or choose from snacks, salads, and tapas at the tasting room. Wines are served by the flight, glass, or bottle. There's beer, too, from Square Wheel Brewing, named for the square-wheeled tractor patented by the estate's original owner, inventor Royal Newton Riblet. Be sure to check out the tractor outside the tasting room and Riblet's oversized garden checkerboard. From May through September, Arbor Crest hosts concerts. It also hosts the Art and Glass Fest, Invitational Class Car Show, weddings, and other special events.

4705 N. Fruit Hill Rd.
509-927-9463
arborcrest.com

TIP
Sample wines from Latah Creek at its Spokane Valley tasting room, just off Interstate 90. Just like Arbor Crest, Latah Creek opened in 1982 and has been crafting a variety of wines ever since, including the popular Huckleberry d'Latah.
13030 E. Indiana Ave., 509-926-0164, latahcreek.com

SPLURGE ON SUNDAY BRUNCH
AT THE DAVENPORT

Walt and Karen Worthy patterned Sunday brunch at the Historic Davenport Hotel after a favorite dining experience: brunch at the Breakers in Palm Beach, Florida. Since they reopened and renovated the landmark downtown hotel in 2002, Sunday brunch at the Davenport has become one of Spokane's quintessential dining experiences. The Isabella Ballroom, the hotel's original dining room, hosts 150 to 200 brunchgoers every week. Reservations triple on holiday weekends and on Sundays in December, when brunch moves to the Grand Pennington Ballroom. Expect bottomless tableside mimosa service, cheese trays, a chilled seafood buffet, and a vast table of desserts, plus a chocolate fountain.

10 S. Post St.
509-789-6848
davenporthotelcollection.com

TIP

Planning to propose? The hotel's Isabella Ballroom, complete with gilded accents, sparkly chandeliers, and a wall of windows reminiscent of the Hall of Mirrors at Versailles, is a picturesque place to pop the question. On the second floor, look for a marriage proposal written underneath a series of reliefs in the hallway. The words "Will you marry me?" were discovered during the hotel's 2002 renovation.

GET A GREAT CUPPA JOE
AT AN INDIE COFFEEHOUSE

Washington state may be the home of Starbucks, but indie coffeehouses rule this western town. In 2018 *National Geographic Traveler* magazine named Spokane one of America's top ten small coffee cities for "the best caffeine fix." You can find good java on nearly every block. Start with the Good Food Award–winning Roast House, which specializes in organic, shade-grown coffees, and its First Avenue Coffee bar, which highlights high-quality, small-batch, and exclusive roasts. Then branch out and visit as many of the city's 150-plus coffee shops and drive-thrus as you can. For addicts, we've highlighted seven standouts that roast their own.

First Avenue Coffee
1017 W. First Ave.
509-201-7091
1stavecoffee.com

Indaba Coffee Roasters
Original: 1425 W. Broadway Ave.
509-443-3566
Downtown: 210 N. Howard St.
509-413-2569
Kendall Yards West: 419 N. Nettleton St.
509-868-0421
Kendall Yards East: 1315 W. Summit Parkway
509-328-4786
Indabacoffee.com

Roast House Coffee
423 E. Cleveland Ave.
509-995-6500
roasthousecoffee.com

Spaceman Coffee
228A W. Sprague Ave.
509-312-9824
spacemancoffeepnw.com

Vessel Coffee Roasters
2823 N. Monroe St.
vesselroasters.com

Doma Coffee Roasters
6240 E. Seltice Way, Post Falls
208-667-1267
domacoffee.com

Evans Brothers Coffee Roasters
504 E. Sherman Ave., Coeur d'Alene
208-930-4065
evansbrotherscoffee.com

SLURP AN OLD-FASHIONED SHAKE
AT THE MILK BOTTLE

It's easy to see where Mary Lou's Milk Bottle got its name. The classic diner is shaped like a giant milk bottle, making it a highly visible fixture in the Garland neighborhood it calls home. You might have caught a glimpse of the Milk Bottle in Johnny Depp's 1993 rom-com *Benny & Joon*. The diner opened around 1933 selling fresh dairy products, and that legacy lives through ice cream churned daily. The food is good, but you'll want to indulge your inner child with a milkshake. Pick your favorite of the twenty-eight flavors, among them River City Sludge and huckleberry. Be prepared to share (or not), because the thick, frothy shake comes with the accompanying overflow in a tin. This $5.75 milkshake is worth every penny.

802 W. Garland Ave.
509-325-1772
marylousmilkbottle.com

TIP
Bring cash or check only; the Milk Bottle does have an ATM.

QUAFF CRAFT BEER AND EAT GREAT GUACAMOLE
AT STEEL BARREL

The Steel Barrel Taproom, downtown Spokane's first brewery incubator, opened in spring 2016 with thirty local, small-batch, and experimental beers on tap—and a specialty food counter to complement those brews. Tucked into the back of the taproom is Zona Blanca, a ceviche eatery owned by Spokane's own *Top Chef* contestant, Chad White. His streamlined menu highlights flavors of coastal Mexico with ceviche-topped tostadas including shrimp and other seafood. Raw fish cured in fresh lime juice may or may not be your thing. Either way, don't miss the guacamole. A large bowl meant for sharing—it pairs well with beer and a group of friends—features lime, cilantro, avocado, habanero, morita chile ash, and a dusting of grasshopper salt.

154 S. Madison St.
509-315-9879 and 509-443-5427
thesteelbarrel.com and limefishsalt.com

TIP
The eatery's cool-looking spice containers with labels that evoke the periodic table come from Spiceology, the Spokane-based spice company. Chad White is a partner, and you can cook like him with Spiceology's chile-lime blend, Cajun blackening blend, and variety of other herbs, salts, spices, and chiles available through spiceology.co.

GRAZE
THE FARMERS MARKET

Spokane's farmers markets overflow with apples, cherries, tomatoes, leafy greens, and other locally grown bounty. Each has a distinct vibe. The bustling Kendall Yards Night Market offers shoppers live music in the Nest, a shipping container turned into a stage overlooking the Spokane River and downtown skyline. The hip Thursday Market in the South Perry District offers a friendly neighborhood feel and cheap beers at the Shop. Morning shoppers might prefer the Spokane Farmers Market in a grassy field near downtown. Look for local specialties including honey, mead, grass-fed meats, foraged morels and chanterelles, blueberries, strawberries, baked goods, hand-blended tea, chai, and gourmet ice pops. Farmers market season runs May through October.

Kendall Yards Night Market
kendallnightmarket.org

Thursday Market in the South Perry District
thursdaymarket.org

Spokane Farmers Market
spokanefarmersmarket.org

TAKE A NOSTALGIC
BURGER TOUR

Go big on your burger choice or don't go at all. The choice here? The Thrifty Scotsman's Super Bacon. Ask for it loaded (a secret that's not on the menu), which adds grilled onions to the already awesome burger that features two patties, rows of crisp bacon, plus lettuce and tomatoes shoved inside a king-sized bun. Throw in a large order of tater tots and a cherry milkshake, and you'll be filled up for days. The Thrifty Scotsman is among the classic burger joints in and around the city that offer a taste of Spokane from a half-century ago. You can enjoy burgers that sound more like carnival rides—the Big R, the Whammy, the Big Dude, and the Big Zipper, just to name a few—in settings that attract some of the area's coolest classic cars.

Thrifty Scotsman Drive In
12024 E. Sprague Ave., Spokane
Valley, 509-928-2214

Dick's Hamburgers
10 E. Third Ave., 509-747-2481

Mike's Burger Royal
6115 E. Trent Ave., Spokane Valley
509-534-3113

Ron's Drive-Inn
12502 E. Sprague Ave., Spokane
Valley, 509-924-6853

Steer Inn
7920 N. Division St., 509-467-6823

Zip's Drive-In
Multiple locations.
Check zipsdrivein.com

WATCH THE PLANES OVER BREAKFAST
AT FELTS FIELD

Pull up a window seat at the Skyway Cafe and feed your inner aviation buff with a meal and a chance to watch airplanes take off and land. The café at Felts Field serves breakfast all day—the house-made sticky buns are famous—and you can find lunch items on the menu, too. The interior is done up in an aviation theme, of course, and celebrates the history of Felts Field, which was Spokane's first airport and first home of the Washington Air National Guard. The terminal, which houses the café, is on the National Register of Historic Places.

6105 E. Rutter Ave.
509-534-5986
skywaycafe.com

DINE BY THE FALLS
AT CLINKERDAGGER

For upscale dining in Spokane, Clinkerdagger has set the standard for more than forty years. Located in the Flour Mill on the north bank of the Spokane River, Clink's dining room features stunning views of the river, Riverfront Park, and downtown. And when the weather's nice, the patio is the place to be. There's a range of steaks, seafood, salads, and pastas for lunch and dinner. One menu favorite is the Broadway Pea Salad, with water chestnuts, bacon, and creamy pepper dressing.

621 W. Mallon Ave.
509-328-5965
clinkerdagger.com

TIP
For another fine-dining option with a river view, check out Anthony's at Spokane Falls. It's part of a regional chain of waterfront restaurants, with a menu featuring steak and seafood.
510 N. Lincoln St., 509-328-9009, anthonys.com

GET A SCOOP
AT THE SCOOP

Coffee and waffles are on the menu, but ice cream is the star. It's made in small batches using liquid nitrogen. You'll find standards such as chocolate, bubble gum, and salted caramel, as well as more adventurous flavors including blueberry lavender, basil, and Fluffer Butter Cup. The Scoop's menu also includes dairy-free, vegan, and gluten-free options and changes frequently, with only a dozen or so flavors available at a time. This family-owned, South Hill neighborhood hangout has indoor and outdoor seating, with bike parking and a spot to leash dogs. The Scoop's vintage ice cream truck is a familiar sight at community events and private gatherings, too.

1001 W. 25th Ave.
509-535-7171
thescoopspokane.com

PADDLE
TO NO-LI BREWHOUSE

Make a date that blends the right mix of activity and ale. After the Spokane River turns into a gentle pool during summer, bring a friend and your stand-up paddleboards to the Division Street Bridge and launch from there. Paddle upstream past the Gonzaga campus and under four bridges. You'll catch glimpses of fish and submerged evidence of the river's industrial past as you go. Soon you'll spy your deserved destination: the outdoor patio and lawn of No-Li, Spokane's largest brewery. Tie up your paddleboards, ascend the bank, and order an award-winning Born & Raised IPA or Wrecking Ball Imperial Stout, just two of the local craft beer offerings. Try an Epic Pretzel with jalapeno cheese sauce. All taste best when enjoyed in a pair of Adirondack chairs overlooking the river.

1003 E. Trent Ave., No. 170
509-242-2739
nolibrewhouse.com

TIP
Use your own paddleboard or rent one at a nearby outdoors shop, such as Flow Adventures or Fun Unlimited.

PICK YOUR OWN
AT GREEN BLUFF

Just north of Spokane, the farming community of Green Bluff is a fun place for family outings to pick apples and pumpkins in the fall. Or to cut down your own Christmas tree in winter. Or to pick cherries, strawberries, and peaches in warm weather months. Local farmers welcome visitors, and you can find an experience that suits your taste. Eleven Acres Farm, for instance, offers you-pick-just-about-anything, including corn, berries, carrots, dill, tomatoes, and beets. Other farms and venues host festivals and fall carnivals with petting zoos, bouncy castles, and bakers selling scrumptious pumpkin doughnuts. Before you go, check the Green Bluff Growers website for a rundown of open orchards and upcoming events.

Info: greenbluffgrowers.com

THROW BACK A SHOT
AT DRY FLY

Smooth. Relaxing. Timeless. The coolest spirit will always be whiskey. Spokane's Dry Fly Distillery makes it in handcrafted batches. The "farm to bottle" distillery, founded in 2007, made its name with its award-winning vodka, but whiskey is where Dry Fly's expertise shines. You'll find several variations: Wheat Whiskey, Bourbon 101, Port Finish, Straight Triticale, and Cask Strength Wheat Whiskey. Visit the tasting room or take a tour on Saturdays to learn how the whiskey is made. You'll also find Dry Fly in downtown establishments. Spokane has a lot to offer, but if you're of age, this is a must taste.

1003 E. Trent Ave.
509-489-2112
dryflydistilling.com

TIP
Sip it neat.

GO GOURMET
WITH GREAT CHEFS

The James Beard Awards recognize culinary excellence, and four area chefs—Jeremy Hansen, Adam Hegsted, Laurent Zirotti, and Anna Vogel—have been honored as semifinalists for Best Chef Northwest. They're an eclectic mix. Vogel's specialty is contemporary Italian cuisine such as ricotta-and-rabbit ravioli and pappardelle lamb ragu. Zirotti owns one of the region's only classic French restaurants; look for Parisian gnocchi, confit de canard, and ris de boeuf sauté au cognac. Hegsted, of the Eat Good Group of restaurants, is known for his whimsical approach to modern American fare and comfort foods, particularly his double-fried chicken with honey-butter. Hansen is known for locally sourced Pacific Northwest fare prepared with traditional French techniques and his ever-changing small plates.

TIP
Zirotti, Hegsted, and Hansen also have less-expensive casual eateries. Zirotti runs Fleur de Sel Artisan Creperie. Hansen has Biscuit Wizard. Hegsted opened a downtown burger joint, Incrediburger and Eggs.

Italia Trattoria (Vogel)
144 S. Cannon St.
509-459-6000
italiatrattoriaspokane.com

Fleur de Sel (Zirotti)
4365 Inverness Drive, Post Falls
208-777-7600
fleur-de-sel.weebly.com

Sante Restaurant and Charcuterie (Hansen)
404 W. Main Ave.
509-315-4613
santespokane.com

Inland Pacific Kitchen (Hansen)
304 W. Pacific Ave.
509-464-6541
ipkspokane.com

Wandering Table (Hegsted)
1242 W. Summit Parkway
509-443-4410
thewanderingtable.com

Honey Eatery and Social Club (Hegsted)
317 Sherman Ave., Coeur d'Alene
208-930-1514
honeyeateryandsocialclub.com

DINE UNDER THE STACKS
AT THE STEAM PLANT

The restaurant at one of Spokane's most iconic properties returned to the downtown dining scene in 2018 after a $4 million renovation. The Steam Plant Kitchen and Brewery has a modern but vintage-inspired, industrial yet elegant vibe. It's located in the 1916 Steam Plant, highly recognizable with its twin stacks rising 225 feet above the city. Designed by renowned Spokane architect Kirtland Cutter, the Steam Plant supplied heat to more than 300 businesses at its peak and operated for nearly seventy years before closing in 1986. It reopened with a restaurant and shops. The menu features wood-fired pizza and rotisserie chicken as well as beer crafted on site. The porchetta sandwich, with arugula, cilantro pesto, and pickled red onion on a toasted ciabatta roll, is a staff favorite.

159 S. Lincoln St.
509-777-3900
steamplantspokane.com

RAISE A TOAST DOWNTOWN
TO WASHINGTON GRAPES

No matter where you are in downtown, you're just a few steps from your next glass of regional wine. Tasting rooms dot the city's center, and you'll find a few winery production facilities, too. Barrister Winery, started by two lawyers, serves up Rough Justice and other award-winning reds at the west edge of downtown. You'll also find Barili Cellars, Bridge Press, V du V Winery, and Robert Karl. (Hint: Don't try to tell your server you know him—Robert Karl isn't a person.) For happy hour before a show downtown, try Terra Blanca. For tastes of Walla Walla wines, check out Cougar Crest and Helix. And in Kendall Yards, visit Maryhill Winery and Craftsman Cellars.

Info: visitspokane.com/cork-district/wineries

SAVOR SPOKANDY

Satisfy your sweet tooth with artisan candies made by Spokane's original candy shop. Founded in 1913, Spokandy creates chocolate-covered creams, caramels, truffles, and huckleberry candies. Don't miss Spokandy's founding sweet, "The Murphy," a vanilla-whipped mallow dipped in chocolate that's still a top seller. Far from mass-factory made, Spokandy produces 150 different candies from recipes handed down for more than a century and hand-crafted by employees who sign agreements not to reveal trade secrets. Shoppers will find gift baskets and novelties like bear claws and chocolate paw prints with almonds, along with mints, seasonal sweets, and a sugar-free line.

1412 W. Third Ave.
509-624-1969
spokandy.com

TIP

Spokane specializes in locally made soft peanut brittle. Bruttles' signature brittle dates back sixty years with a recipe from Aunt Sophia Gerkensmeyer, who hand-pulled her brittle on a marble slab. The Historic Davenport Hotel also makes an in-house old-fashioned brittle using a marble slab. You'll find both brittles—at the Historic Davenport and Bruttles—selling across the street from each other on Sprague Avenue downtown.

FOLLOW IN THE FOOTSTEPS
OF JIMMIE DURKIN

James Durkin was an Irish immigrant who landed in New York in 1868, ran away at age nine, and got a job at a Brooklyn bar at thirteen. Eventually, he made his way west to Spokane, where he operated three saloons and made a fortune as a liquor distributor. A restaurant and bar named after this colorful local legend—Durkin's Liquor Bar—still thrives downtown, serving cocktails and elevated pub fare. The burger is one of the best in town, and the fried bologna sandwich, made from house-made bologna, is a local favorite. The drinks menu is creative and always interesting—the Black Friday sports vodka, beet syrup, lime, ginger, honey, and, yes, activated charcoal.

415 W. Main Ave.
509-863-9501
durkinsliquorbar.com

TIP
Try a whiskey with a pickle back—one shot of whiskey and one shot of pickle brine. It's not the green stuff from a jar of store-bought dills. They make their own pickles at Durkin's, and the brine is oniony and delightful.

ENJOY UPSCALE FOOD
AT A GAS STATION

Hay J's Bistro is located in a gas-station strip mall in Liberty Lake. But don't let that stop you from dining at this little gem of a restaurant named in honor of the chef's children, Haley and Jackson. The exterior is unassuming, to say the least. Inside, Hay J's offers an extensive wine list and innovative contemporary cuisine with Mediterranean and Asian influences. Start with ponzu calamari or ahi tuna tartare, and then look for a variety of plentiful salads, pasta dishes, and entrees such as pork chops with mustard greens, Chilean sea bass with coconut curry sauce and sticky rice, and Parmesan-crusted halibut. Reservations are recommended.

21706 E. Mission Ave., Liberty Lake
509-926-2310
hayjsbistro.com

FEAST
AT KENDALL YARDS

This newer neighborhood runs along the north bank of the Spokane River and offers magnificent views of the downtown skyline. So do most of its eateries, and you'll find lots of tasty options. Consider thin-crust, wood-fired pizza on the patio at Veraci, or beer or wine next door at Nectar. Central Food offers entrees such as pan-seared Idaho trout, local lentils, and, at lunch, a killer Korean pork sandwich. Don't forget to pick up a loaf of house-made, naturally leavened bread to go. Umi Kitchen and Sushi specializes in seafood, Japanese cuisine, and Asian-inspired craft cocktails. Park Lodge, open for dinner, specializes in Pacific Northwest fare with Mediterranean and Middle Eastern influences. It shares a building with the mini-doughnut-and-coffee shop Hello Sugar and Indaba.

FOLLOW
THE ALE TRAIL

The Northwest is known as a craft beer hotbed, and the Spokane area boasts thirty-odd breweries stretching in every direction. To the west, a budding downtown brewery district is anchored by Iron Goat (try the Blackberry Apricot Sour) and up-and-comer Whistle Punk. To the east, a burgeoning Valley scene ranges from pioneering Twelve String (think hoppy IPAs and barrel-aged beers) to classy newcomer Millwood Brewing. Up north, it's the likes of Bellwether (specializing in Old World styles with honey and herbs) and Green Bluff's farm-based Big Barn. South of the freeway you'll find Perry Street Brewing (rock-solid classic styles) and the Grain Shed brewery/bakery co-op, using regionally grown ancient grains. And local leader No-Li's beers show up all over town in bottles, cans, and draft.

Info: inlandnwaletrail.com.

TIP
The Inland Northwest Craft Beer Festival is in September. Year round plan your Inland Northwest Ale Trail visits with the handy map available at breweries. Or download it from the website.

ORDER A STEAK TO REMEMBER
AT WOLF LODGE INN

If you're looking for a memorable meal and want to ditch the city for some fresh air, try Wolf Lodge Inn. Tucked in the hills just outside Coeur d'Alene, the restaurant is a fifty-minute drive from downtown Spokane, and you'll catch gorgeous views of Lake Coeur d'Alene along the ride. Wolf Lodge's atmosphere is casual and country, featuring plenty of woodsy, Old West décor. The menu is simple steakhouse fare with ample portions. Don't mistake simple for low quality. The meat is seasoned and cooked to perfection over a tamarack fire. Steak lovers should make the journey. Don't bring vegetarians.

11741 E. Frontage Rd., Coeur d'Alene
208-664-6665
wolflodgesteakhouse.com

TIP

In downtown Spokane, Churchill's Steakhouse serves up premium cuts in a classic steakhouse atmosphere. Downstairs in the bar, enjoy a Huckleberry Lemondrop as a piano player performs seven nights a week.

165 S. Post St., 509-474-9888
churchillssteakhouse.com

TAKE IN
THE TINY TIKI BAR

The Tiny Tiki, an intimate South Pacific–themed rum bar, opened downtown in 2018 and stretches fewer than 500 square feet. The menu, like the space, is streamlined. Expect classic tiki drinks, such as the Painkiller, as well as a rum-forward full bar. Don't leave without trying the signature drink. The Tiny Tiki specializes in mai tais not only on tap but on nitro. Grab a cocktail and get cozy on shag-covered benches separated by Polynesian-inspired screens under bamboo framework replicating an A-frame hut. Faux foliage above the bar and Japanese fish floats and lanterns on the ceiling round out the experience.

307 W. Second Ave.
thetinytiki.com

STROLL
THE PERRY DISTRICT

The stretch of South Perry Street between 9th and 13th avenues offers a smorgasbord for foodies. The best part: everything is within walking distance. Try the popular Perry Street Brewing for a pint plus street-style tacos, fancy toasts, and cheese-and-charcuterie boards. More pub grub is available at the Lantern Taphouse across the street. South Perry Pizza offers artisan pies. Casper Fry focuses on upscale Southern-inspired fare, including an elevated take on fried chicken, molasses-brined pork chops, and shrimp and grits. The bustling Thursday Market in the South Perry District is held in the parking lot of the Shop, a café and coffee shop. And check out the Grain Shed, which features loaves made from locally grown grain milled on site and baked in a custom wood-fired oven.

MUSIC AND ENTERTAINMENT

LUXURIATE IN ART DECO SPLENDOR
AT THE FOX

It doesn't matter who's on stage, it's always a feast for the eyes at the Martin Woldson Theater at the Fox. It's the home of the Spokane Symphony and also hosts rock, jazz, comedy, and dance troupes in style. The symphony's home stage came back to life in 2007 after renovations to restore the Art Deco murals and starburst light and update electrical and plumbing systems. The downtown landmark originally opened as a movie house in 1931 and was Spokane's first air-conditioned building. After decades hosting movies and stage shows—including performances by Katharine Hepburn, Frank Sinatra, and Spokane's own Bing Crosby—the theater fell into disrepair as a second-run movie house. In 2000, it was slated for demolition until a community campaign raised $30 million to save the Fox. There isn't a bad seat in the house.

1001 W. Sprague Ave.
509-624-1200
foxtheaterspokane.org

PIG OUT
IN THE PARK

When prepping for Pig Out in the Park, there are two things to consider: What do you want to eat, and who do you want to see perform? Over the course of the festival's four decades downtown, Pig Out has become equally known for its food offerings (forty-seven food booths, more than two hundred menu items, three adult beverage gardens) and its eclectic concert lineup (dozens of local, regional, and national artists on three stages). The summer 2018 edition featured Heartland rockers BoDeans of "Closer to Free" fame; alt-rock band Dishwalla, best known for the single "Counting Blue Cars"; and hip-hop duo Kid 'n Play, known as much for its work on screen as its music. Admission is free.

Riverfront Park, 507 N. Howard St.
509-921-5579
spokanepigout.com

IMBIBE AN ADULT BEVERAGE
AT BABY BAR

Baby Bar is best known for its signature cocktail—a Greyhound made with freshly pressed grapefruit juice—and for having the best jukebox in town. Patrons play the Misfits, Pixies, Pogues, and Violent Femmes at this punk-rock hole-in-the-wall, where it's always dark no matter the time of day. Seating is limited. If it gets too crowded, look for a spot at the adjacent Neato Burrito, where you also can grab a late-night burrito or plate of nachos, take in a poetry open mic night, or watch an alt-rock or punk show. There's beer on tap in both spots. But Baby Bar has the red lights and "Twin Peaks"-inspired décor. Singer-songwriter Neko Case once tweeted: "The Baby Bar in Spokane, WA. Best bar in USA. No question." So put another dollar in the jukebox, baby.

827 W. First Ave.
509-847-1234
Online: Search "Baby Bar Spokane" on Facebook

CATCH A CLASSIC
AT THE GARLAND

Except for a few brief closures, the Garland Theater has been a Spokane mainstay since opening in 1945. Now a discount theater seating 500, the Garland is a throwback to a bygone era before reclining seats and $15 tickets. It's the perfect place to see a classic film. With a varied menu of snacks and the option to order beer and wine, it pleases adults and children alike. During summer the Garland shows family-friendly movies one night a week. For the more adventurous, catch a midnight show of cult classics like *The Rocky Horror Picture Show* and *The Room*. Whatever you decide to see, at $5 a movie (or $2.50 on Wednesdays!), your wallet will thank you.

924 W. Garland Ave.
509-327-2509; 509-327-1050 (showtimes)
garlandtheater.com

TIP
Get there early and enjoy a drink at the Bon Bon, the Garland's lounge, which offers happy-hour specials and trivia nights.

PAINT THE TOWN
AT SUMMER ART FESTIVALS

Summer in the Inland Northwest is bookmarked by two outdoor art festivals. First up, in June, is Spokane's ArtFest, which brings art, music, and food to Browne's Addition. The three-day festival, presented by the Northwest Museum of Arts and Culture, features more than 150 juried artists who share ceramics, drawing, fiber, glass, jewelry, leather, metal work, painting, photography, printmaking, and wood. Every August, in Coeur d'Alene, Art on the Green brings a wide range of art plus food and music to North Idaho College. More than 190 artists share handcrafted pieces in glass, clay, leather, wood, metal, and fiber at the three-day festival. Both festivals have stations where children can create art.

ArtFest: Coeur d'Alene Park
2195 W. Second Ave., 509-456-3931
artfestspokane.com

Art on the Green: North Idaho College
1000 W. Garden Ave., Coeur d'Alene, 208-667-9346
artonthegreencda.com

SEE BIG-NAME TALENT
AT THE BING

It's not the biggest theater in town (the INB Performing Arts Center) nor the most elegant (the Fox Theater). But it is the most Spokane of them all. Even the theater's name knows it: The Bing. The Bing Crosby Theater isn't just named after one of Spokane's most famous artists; he actually performed there in 1925 before becoming a national household name. The beautifully restored 750-seat venue offers an eclectic mix of acts that ranges from local community theater groups to first-tier comedians to your favorite bands from college. It's a great place to see a show, especially a big-name act that typically plays in much bigger halls. Which happens more often than you'd expect. In recent years, Macklemore and Ryan Lewis, Fred Armisen, Lucinda Williams, Robert Cray, and the Avett Brothers have played the Bing. Even Pearl Jam, then on the cusp of superstardom, made a memorable stop there in 1993.

901 W. Sprague Ave.
509-227-7638
bingcrosbytheater.com

EXPERIENCE A COLLISION OF ART AND MUSIC
AT TERRAIN

When Terrain co-founders Ginger Ewing and Luke Baumgarten and friends organized the first Terrain in 2008, they hoped the event would inspire young artists to stay in town. Thirty artists submitted work, which about 1,200 people took in. A decade later, Terrain 10 attracted more than 300 artists, and 8,500 people attended the show. Perhaps the best thing about Terrain is that you never know what you're going to see. Artists have displayed everything from realistic large-scale paintings of pieces of meat (Ryan Desmond) and a Radio Flyer made to look like it was using hydraulics (Juventino Aranda) to a cape of sorts covered with family heirlooms (Lou Lou Pink) and woodcut relief prints (Reinaldo Alexander Gil Zambrano). This annual art party is traditionally held the first Friday in October, in conjunction with the city's Fall Visual Arts Tour.

Washington Cracker Building, 304 W. Pacific Ave.
terrainspokane.com

SING AND DANCE ON THE BAR
AT O'DOHERTY'S

O'Doherty's Irish Grille in downtown Spokane has the hallmark sights and smells of an Old Country pub—corned beef and cabbage, plenty of Guinness, and a quorum of regular patrons. But it's the venue's approach to interior decoration that sets it apart. The walls are papered with thousands of dollar bills, each bearing a different signature. Owner Tim O'Doherty declines to say how many, but considering the tradition started in the early '90s, you can be sure there are several decades' worth of good times tacked up there. Adding your name to the tableau is the fun part. The rules are simple: Pick a song, any song. Climb onto the bar. Belt it out. Your name goes on a dollar, the dollar goes on the wall, and you become part of the extended O'Doherty's clan.

525 W. Spokane Falls Blvd.
509-747-0322
odohertyspub.com

TIP
Consider taking to the stage—er, bar—sooner rather than later. Aside from everlasting fame and the satisfaction of a song well sung, performing at the pub gets you half off your first drink during every visit for the rest of your life.

GO TO A GLORIOUS CONCERT
AT THE CATHEDRAL

The Cathedral of St. John the Evangelist is a towering example of Gothic architecture perched on Spokane's South Hill. The Episcopal congregation that worships there happily shares its gorgeous building with the public for a host of musical and cultural events. The Northwest BachFest typically holds its finale in the church, and St. John's has hosted performances by such diverse performers as the Spokane Youth Symphony, the Spokane String Quartet, pianist and radio host Christopher O'Riley, and Grammy-winning cellist Zuill Bailey. The church houses a 4,000-pipe organ, a 1961 Aeolian-Skinner, and a carillon with 49 cast bells. The carillon is best heard from outside, and it is played weekly before the Sunday 10:30 a.m. service.

127 E. 12th Ave.
509-838-4277
stjohns-cathedral.org

TIP

On July 4, head up the South Hill, grab a spot on the lawn outside St. John's Cathedral before dusk, and take in a free carillon concert that leads up to the annual fireworks display over downtown. Beautiful music and a view!

TAKE IN A SMALL CLUB WITH BIG IDEAS
AT THE BARTLETT

With string lights above the stage and exposed brick, you'd be hard pressed to find a cozier venue than The Bartlett. The almost always all-ages venue (children 8 and younger get in free) has been a local favorite since Caleb and Karli Ingersoll opened the 150-person-capacity club in 2013. Save for a support beam, the floor is nice and open, which makes dancing easy, and benches line the walls for when you need a minute to rest. The folks at The Bartlett book an eclectic mix of veteran and up-and-coming national artists, while also making sure to highlight the Inland Northwest's talent pool through events like open mic nights, poetry slams, and variety shows featuring country, soul, folk, and bluegrass (Northwest of Nashville) and jazz (Northwest of New Orleans).

228 W. Sprague Ave.
509-747-2174
thebartlettspokane.com

ROCK OUT
AT THE KNIT

One of the few mid-sized venues in town, the 1,500-person-capacity Knitting Factory is a downtown staple. The Knit hosts both national touring acts and local musicians, and over the years it's become a regular stop for many an out-of-town artist (read: Tech N9ne). Tickets usually run between $15 and $35, so a night at the Knit won't cost you an arm and a leg, though the venue also regularly hosts free "Too Broke to Rock" concerts. Unless a show is sold out, there's usually plenty of space to shimmy on the floor, and those who want to enjoy a drink during the show can watch from the 21-and-over sections. The Knit offers annual passes that include admission for two to every show at the venue.

919 W. Sprague Ave.
509-244-3279
sp.knittingfactory.com

TIP
For the best spot, those 21 and older should grab a drink or bite to eat at the Knit's restaurant, the District Bar, which opens at 4 p.m. Diners then get into the venue before the general public. Be sure to make a reservation.

GET DOWN
WITH BACH AND BEETHOVEN

Spokane's Connoisseur Concerts has hosted the Northwest BachFest each winter since 1978. Cellist Zuill Bailey took over in 2013 as artistic director, replacing Pulitzer Prize–winning composer and conductor Gunther Schuller when he retired. Since then, the festival has expanded from a two-week event to offer programming throughout the year. Look for free luncheon concerts, called Bach's Lunch. And pop-up performances, Flash Bach, in bank and hotel lobbies. And thought-provoking performances in wineries, school gymnasiums, and other unexpected locations. The festival brings world-class musicians to Spokane, Coeur d'Alene, and Walla Walla. The season includes Mozart on a Summer's Eve in Manito Park in July, a SummerFest series in August, and Winter Classics in December, in addition to the festival in February and March.

509-326-4942
nwbachfest.com

SOAK UP SUMMERTIME
IN SANDPOINT

About seventy miles from Spokane, on the shores of Lake Pend Oreille in the Idaho Panhandle, is Sandpoint, a year-round hub of recreation. Since 1983, the city has been home to the Festival at Sandpoint, where big-name performers such as Willie Nelson, Johnny and June Carter Cash, Brandi Carlile, Chris Isaak, Rickie Lee Jones, Pink Martini, and the Head and the Heart have played under the stars. Held over two weeks in August, the festival brings an eclectic mix of pop, country, blues, classic, and rock acts to the region. The venue holds about 4,000 people, so festival goers can enjoy a more intimate experience than at a stadium show.

208-265-4554
festivalatsandpoint.com

RING IN THE NEW YEAR
FOR THE SYMPHONY

If you're looking to end, or start, the year on an especially classy note, consider attending "Puttin' on the Ritz," the Spokane Symphony's annual fundraiser. The black-tie event features a paparazzi-lined runway and includes a multi-course dinner, plus salad and dessert, and a no-host bar at the Historic Davenport Hotel. After dinner, dance to the music from Master Class Big Band and participate in door-prize drawings. When the countdown begins, ring in the new year with a glass of champagne and party favors. The party continues until 1 a.m. so you can dance your way into the new year. "Puttin' on the Ritz" is popular, so be sure to check for tickets as December draws near.

Davenport Historic Hotel, 10 S. Post St.
spokanesymphony.org or ticketswest.com

PARTY FOR A CAUSE
AT GLEASON FEST

Going to watch live music is fun. Getting to watch live music and help out a good cause? Even better. The annual Gleason Fest was inspired by Spokane's own Steve Gleason, a former NFL player who was diagnosed with amyotrophic lateral sclerosis (ALS) in 2011. Proceeds from the summer festival go to the Gleason Initiative Foundation, which provides life-improving technology and services to those afflicted with ALS and raises awareness about the disease. Team Gleason aims to inspire others with the disease not only to live, but to thrive. Much in that same vein, Gleason Fest is more than a chance to donate. It's a chance to celebrate life with great live music in the Lilac Bowl Amphitheatre at Riverfront Park.

507 N. Howard St.
gleasonfest.org

Photo credit: Jesse Tinsley

SPORTS AND RECREATION

THRILL TO A FANTASTIC
SKYRIDE

Spokane has waterfalls, and waterfalls can be dangerous. What better way to evade danger and get as close as possible to the falls than on a gondola in the air? The SkyRide begins in a calm setting: in Riverfront Park, right in the center of the city, not far from the shaved-ice booth. Within minutes of entering the many-windowed cabin, gondoliers are quite literally dangling and swinging over the roaring whitewater of the lower falls. Your heart will beat a bit faster. Your camera will shoot a lot faster. The whole thing takes about fifteen minutes. And how about that Monroe Street Bridge framing everything, eh?

507 N. Howard St.
509-625-6600
my.spokanecity.org/riverfrontpark/attractions/skyride/

TIP
Ride in May. Or April. Or as early as possible to see the river at its most swollen when the snowmelt tumbles furiously down the falls.

PHOTOGRAPH A MOOSE
IN CITY LIMITS

Spokane is among just a few cities in the nation that is home to moose. The largest of the deer species has found its way into city parks, streets, and backyard swimming pools; one moose calf had to be rescued after crashing through a window into the basement of a North Side home. Aspire to join the ranks of Spokanites and visitors who have sent friends and relatives photos of moose in the city. Increase odds of seeing one of the 700-pound chocolate brown critters by paddling the Little Spokane River or hiking the county's Iller Creek Conservation Area trails in Spokane Valley. Or simply keep the camera or smartphone handy. Skip the selfies. Unpredictable moose can go from docile to defensive in a heartbeat.

Spokanecounty.org

TIP
Do not approach a moose. If its ears suddenly flatten down to its head, you've gone too far and it might be too late!

TUBE
THE SPOKANE RIVER

Lazy summer days are best spent on the river. Luckily for you, Spokane's got a river running through it. First, you need a tube. The White Elephant, Spokane's longtime outdoor gear store, sells them for less than $20. You'll find numerous places to put in and take out; one nice option is starting in Peaceful Valley at the Glover Field boat launch, at West Main Avenue and North Cedar Street. From there, float to the T. J. Meenach Bridge. Within minutes you'll find yourself in a peaceful and scenic landscape reminiscent of a wilder river. But be careful. Don't overshoot the takeout, as the river gets wilder and more technical after the bridge. And wear a lifejacket.

TIP
Visit spokaneriver.net/watertrail for a full list of river activities.

SNAG THE HOTTEST TICKET IN TOWN
AT GONZAGA

Before all of the trips to the Sweet Sixteen and Final Four, there wasn't a lot of demand for Gonzaga University basketball tickets. When the 6,000-seat McCarthey Athletic Center opened in 2004, it seemed plenty big. It's not. The Zags could easily sell twice as many tickets to most games. When you add that the team rarely loses on its home court, making the Kennel the winningest arena in the sports world, it's easy to see why every game sells out. So how do you get tickets? Here are your three best chances: See a game in December when the students are on break, though the atmosphere isn't nearly as electric without the students. Join the Bulldog Club, which costs about $250 annually, to increase your chances of scoring tickets. Check out the secondary ticket market, like Craigslist and other online ticket sites, where individual tickets cost anywhere from $100 to more than $500.

Gonzaga University, McCarthey Athletics Center
801 N. Cincinnati St.
509-313-6000
gozags.com

TAKE A SPIN
ON THE LOOFF CARROUSEL

With its fifty-four hand-painted and hand-carved wooden horses, one giraffe, one tiger, and two Chinese dragon chairs, the Looff Carrousel is one of Riverfront Park's signature attractions. It was built in 1909 by famed designer Charles I.D. Looff and is now listed on the National Register of Historic Places as one of the most beautiful carousels of its kind. In 2018 the restored Looff Carrousel reopened downtown in a new, jewelry-box-inspired $7 million setting. It's spinning again and open daily for $2 rides from 10 a.m. to 7 p.m. Kids can try to grab a golden plastic ring as they glide around, which earns them a free ride. They can then fling it at a vinyl reproduction of the nearby Garbage Goat to recycle the ring.

507 N. Howard St.
509-625-6600
my.spokanecity.org/riverfrontpark/attractions/looff-carrousel/

TIP
Stick around Riverside Park for more fun, including free yoga on the nearby Howard Street Bridge. Kids can run through the recently renovated Rotary Fountain on hot summer afternoons.

SLIDE DOWN
THE BIG RED WAGON

No, your eyes aren't deceiving you. That is a giant Radio Flyer wagon in Spokane's Riverfront Park. Called the *Childhood Express*, it was created for the Centennial Celebration of Children by local artist Ken Spiering in 1989 and weighs 26 tons. And though it may have had the title of world's largest red wagon stripped by a behemoth dedicated in Chicago for the longtime wagon-maker's centennial birthday, Spokane's version boasts a twenty-foot slide. It also has monkey bars underneath that make it tough to pull the kids (and amateur thrill-seekers) away.

507 N. Howard St.
509-625-6600
my.spokanecity.org/riverfrontpark/highlights/red-wagon/

SKATE
THE ICE RIBBON

Zip around Spokane's skating ribbon, the only attraction of its kind on the West Coast. For a skating experience different than your typical trip to the rink, Riverfront Park's skating ribbon offers new thrills. Opened in December 2017, the ribbon is 645 feet long and features a three-foot change in elevation that will have you shooting around corners and climbing back to the adjacent SkyRibbon Café for a hot chocolate warmup. Bring your own skates to avoid the lines and a $4.50 charge for rentals. In warmer months, you can hang up your ice skates and put on some wheels.

507 N. Howard St.
509-625-6600
my.spokanecity.org/riverfrontpark/attractions/skate-ribbon

TIP
Fans of ice skating and hockey also will enjoy the Spokane Chiefs' Teddy Bear Toss Night in December when fans fill the ice with thousands of stuffed bears to benefit needy kids during the holidays.
spokanechiefs.com

HIT THE STREETS
FOR HOOPFEST

What do you need to play in the largest three-on-three basketball tournament on Earth? A couple of your tallest friends would be a good start, along with a clever team name (Cookies and Kareem?) and a few pairs of fresh socks. Featuring 25,000 players and 3,000 volunteers spread over 450 courts filling the streets of downtown Spokane, Hoopfest takes place the last weekend of June. It includes divisions for all skill and age levels: wheelchair, youth, family, co-ed, and elite. The street game tends to get a little heated, both from a temperature and temperament standpoint, so stay hydrated and stay cool. Remember: Unless you're in the elite division, you can only win a T-shirt.

421 W. Riverside Ave., Suite 115
509-624-2414
spokanehoopfest.net

TIP
If you're coming from out of town, reserve a hotel room early. They fill up quickly. The window for Hoopfest registration starts in early March and ends in late May.

RUN BLOOMSDAY

On the first Sunday of every May, runners, walkers, and people in wheelchairs pack seven blocks of Riverside Avenue for Bloomsday, one of the world's largest road races. The 40,000-plus participants include serious runners, but make no mistake, Bloomsday is open to anyone willing to train for it. The twelve-kilometer course is lined with rock bands, accordion players, church choirs, candidates for office, and young Otter Pop salespeople. Past the halfway mark, "Bloomies," as runners are called, head up what's known as Doomsday Hill. When you make it to the top, you are rewarded with an encounter with the ten-foot Bloomsday vulture, which has greeted participants every year since 1987. At the final turn, speakers blast "Chariots of Fire" as you complete the last blocks downhill.

Info: 509-838-1579. Bloomsdayrun.org

TIP
From Ironman competitions to the Bare Buns Fun Run to the Valley Girl Triathlon, Spokane is a hub for walks, runs, and races of all types. Find your next event: runningintheusa.com/race/list/map/within-50-miles-of-spokane-wa/

PITCH IN
AT A RIVER CLEAN-UP

Spokane's signature attraction draws all sorts of creatures, including beavers, snakes, caddisflies, and some litterbugs, too. The annual Spokane River Clean-up is a fun and effective way to pay respect to the natural feature other cities would love to have. About 600 people spend a September morning in friendly competition to see which team can gather the most trash. Kids beam like they just caught a trophy trout when they help drag a pickup bumper off the shoreline. The group effort relieves the river banks from tons of junk. Register with a group or as an individual.

Info: spokaneriver.net/spokanerivercleanup/

PLAY CATCH ON THE FIELD
AT AN INDIANS GAME

Avista Stadium, home to the Spokane Indians baseball team, typically ranks as one of the best minor league parks. It's not the newest or the shiniest or even in a great location. But it's definitely filled with charm. And one of the most charming things you can do at the stadium happens after Sunday afternoon games. That's when fans are allowed on the outfield after the game to play catch. Though the field looks great from the stands, it's even more amazing when you're standing on it. With your glove. Playing catch with family or friends. The field is softer than you imagined and greener than you realized. Playing catch is fun, but playing a game of catch on an immaculately manicured professional baseball field is something you'll never forget.

602 N. Havana St.
509-343-6886
milb.com/spokane

ZIP ACROSS
MICA PEAK

A thrilling way to see Spokane Valley is hanging from a harness and a metal cable as you race thirty-eight mph toward a tree. Mica Moon Zip Tours combines some of the most majestic views of the area with an adrenaline rush of speed, heights, and excitement. Take your pick of eight zip-line runs, including "Major Tom," "Point of No Return," and "White Lightning." Owners Rik and Heidi Stewart created a combination business and thrill park out of 200 acres of family ground that has remnants of cabins dating back to Prohibition.

Mica Moon Zip Tours
23403 E. Mission Ave. No. 111, Liberty Lake
509-587-4020
micamoon.com

TIP
In 2018 Mica Moon added a three-acre aerial park that allows urban adventurers to test their skills on challenge courses, such as high-rise tight ropes, canoe and wine barrel bridges, and nets suspended thirty to seventy feet above ground connecting to tree platforms.

JOIN THE DAWN PATROL
AT MOUNT SPOKANE

Tired of the lines, limitations, and costs of resort skiing? Then get up early and ski Mount Spokane. Just an hour from downtown, Spokane's namesake mountain opens for uphill travel at 6:30 a.m. You can catch a sunrise and beat the crowds on the slopes. Start at Mount Spokane Ski and Snowboard Resort lodge 1, the first chairlift you pass driving up. Travel uphill, following the outside edge of the groomed trail to the Tea Kettle junction, and continue to the summit. Your legs will burn and your heart may race from the effort of skiing uphill. But reaching the summit and starting the descent makes any sweat spent well worth the effort. At 9:10 a.m. uphill skiers ski down. And if you're blessed with a clear day, the views of Spokane, North Idaho, and the Cabinet Mountains in Montana are breathtaking. Early morning skiing is free, if you have the uphill gear, or you can rent it.

29500 N. Mt. Spokane Park Drive, Mead
509-238-2220
mtspokane.com/uphill-travel-policy

TIP

In addition to Mount Spokane, you can ski or snowboard at four other ski areas within a two-hour drive of downtown Spokane. Check out 49 Degrees North inside Colville National Forest; Schweitzer Mountain Resort in Sandpoint, Idaho; Silver Mountain in Kellogg, Idaho; and Lookout Pass on the Idaho/Montana border.

PADDLE
THE LITTLE SPOKANE RIVER

Spending an afternoon canoeing or kayaking the Little Spokane River can make you forget the world. Songbirds, herons, ducks, and painted turtles share this serpentine stretch of water north of town. Start your journey near St. George's School, the best and most accessible put-in spot. You can bring your own equipment or rent it for the day. Plan to spend at least two to three hours on this small river, paddling your way to the developed takeout near the confluence with the Spokane River. No summer or fall should go by without this close and rewarding trip.

Info: Rent canoes or kayaks at Mountain Gear or REI,
two of the city's main outdoor gear shops.

TIP
If this is your first time, check a guidebook for trip planning and specifics. Our favorite: *Paddle Routes of the Inland Northwest* by Rich Landers and Dan Hansen.

HOOK UP
WITH A TROUT

Fly fishing for redbands is a local angle into the past, present, and future of the Spokane River. This handsome subspecies of rainbow trout, with brick-red streaks on its sides and splashed with black freckling, is a native with lineage dating back thousands of years. Casting an imitation bug and hearing the scream of line peeling off a reel connects you with the fish and its environment. A state fishing license is required; the season runs June to March, and the trout must be immediately released alive. Watching it swim out of the net to carry on the species is the best part.

TIP
Learn fly-fishing skills and where to catch redbands with classes and guided trips offered by local fly-fishing outfitters, such as Silver Bow Fly Shop.
13210 E. Indiana Ave., Spokane Valley, 509-924-9998
silverbowflyshop.com

WALK
THE CENTENNIAL TRAIL

If you visit Spokane, there's a good chance you'll find yourself on the Centennial Trail. More than 2 million people do it each year, and it's an enjoyable place for a quiet bike ride or walk. For sixty miles the paved trail follows the contours of the Spokane River. It meanders beneath the basalt cliffs northwest of the city, the thundering waterfalls of downtown, the lazy welcoming water in Spokane Valley, and the forests and lakes of Post Falls and Coeur d'Alene. A water bottle and comfortable shoes are all you need for a perfect day.

Info: spokanecentennialtrail.org

PLAY THE CANYON

If the gorgeous design and panoramic views of Spokane from the clubhouse and first and tenth tee boxes aren't enough reason to visit Indian Canyon, how about the chance to walk the same lush fairways once strolled by legends Byron Nelson, Sam Snead, and Ben Hogan? This venerable city course has been ranked among the nation's finest public courses and hosted several PGA and USGA tournaments. The challenging layout includes striking elevation changes, tree-lined fairways, and slippery undulating greens. Hogan once called No. 8, a par 3 that can stretch to 224 yards, the most demanding single-shot hole he'd ever played. It's affordable (roughly $40), and the view from the veranda overlooking the city while enjoying a post-round beverage is worth every penny.

1000 S. Assembly Road
509-747-5353
my.spokanecity.org/golf/courses/indian-canyon

TIP
Try to stay below the pin on approach shots. Nearly all of Indian Canyon's greens are wavy and/or tiered, and putting from above the hole could add strokes to your score.

BRAVE THE TIMBER TERROR
AT SILVERWOOD

The second roller coaster to join Silverwood Theme Park's fleet of thrill rides and the first of the wooden variety, Timber Terror is for parkgoers who like their derrieres in the air. The simple out-and-back track design that gives you views of the coaster's brethren throughout the park maximizes the feeling of weightlessness with a high-waist safety bar and several sharp drops and tight turns. Queasy types may want to skip the corn dogs before this one.

27843 N. Hwy 95, Athol, Idaho
208-683-3400
silverwoodthemepark.com/

TIP
If you've already made the plunge on this wooden thriller and can relive the bunny hills with your eyes closed, consider attending the annual Halloween event "Scarywood," when the cars are reversed and riders experience the terror backward.

FIND A SWIMMING HOLE

In 2018, the city of Spokane made it easy to cool off: Admission to city pools and splash pads is now free. Or, if you want to dive into wild waters, the region offers excellent swimming holes. Here are some of the best: In Spokane, head to Boulder Beach on the north shore of the Spokane River adjacent to Camp Sekani Park. You'll also find sandy beaches at Coeur d'Alene City Park and Yap-Keehn-Um Beach, which borders North Idaho College. The two beaches stretch from downtown Coeur d'Alene to the mouth of the Spokane River. More adventurous swimmers will want to head just down the shore to Tubbs Hill. It's full of little beaches and giant rocks to jump off, plus a hiking trail, too. It's a sight to witness the single-minded athletes run their hearts out.

City pools
my.spokanecity.org/recreation/aquatics/

Swimming holes
visitspokane.com/things-to-do/waterways/swimming-beaches/

TAKE A BALD EAGLE TOUR
AT LAKE COEUR D'ALENE

They're big, bold, and beautiful, and they flock to Lake Coeur d'Alene every winter. Watch bald eagles swoop and soar in their hunt for spawning kokanee salmon. A forty-five-minute drive from Spokane, this natural spectacle can't be missed. Prime watching time is between November and the third week of December. In 2017, observers counted 372 bald eagles here, setting a new record. The best viewpoints are Higgins Point, Mineral Ridge, and Beauty Bay. All three are east of Coeur d'Alene and easily accessible by car. Coeur d'Alene Lake Cruises also offers eagle-watching trips.

Info: cdacruises.com/daily-cruises/eagles/
visitnorthidaho.com

CROSS A SUSPENSION BRIDGE
AT THE BOWL AND PITCHER

Riverside State Park is one of Spokane's best nature getaways. And no place in the park is better than the suspension bridge that crosses Spokane River whitewater near the massive basalt features called the Bowl and Pitcher. The bridge gives walkers a lump-in-the-throat thrill as it lifts and eases over the fast-moving river. It links the parking and picnic area of the state park with the trail system that courses through the forest. You'll find wildflowers, birds, river views, and other walkers who know, just like you do, that the suspension bridge and its access to the best of the park is an adventure that beckons newcomers and longtime residents again and again.

9711 W. Charles Road, Nine Mile Falls
509-465-5064
parks.state.wa.us/573/riverside

WALK DUNCAN GARDENS
AT MANITO PARK

Established in 1904 and once home to a zoo, this landmark public park is one of Spokane's best places to picnic and pose for photographs. Expansive grounds cover ninety acres filled with rose and lilac gardens, a conservatory, an arboretum, and playgrounds. The Mirror Pond is a great place to watch ducks and other water fowl, and, when it freezes over in winter, neighborhood kids and adults play hockey here. Duncan Garden is a popular spot for weddings. Be sure to visit the giant koi in the park's gated Japanese garden.

1702 S. Grand Blvd.
509-625-6200
my.spokanecity.org/parks/major/manito/

TIP

Grab a coffee and pastry at Rockwood Bakery, across the street, and head to the park for a walk or light picnic. The café and coffee shop is known for its house-made pie, quiche, cupcakes, cookies, and other baked goods, as well as sandwiches and salads. Inside the park, nosh at the Park Bench Cafe, which has live music during summer.

TAKE A HIKE
AND GET A GOOEY
AT TUBBS HILL

Right in the middle of downtown Coeur d'Alene is Tubbs Hill, a 165-acre publicly owned slice of nature jutting out into Lake Coeur d'Alene. The hill is perched adjacent to the newly redeveloped McEuen Park and the iconic Coeur d'Alene Resort. Tubbs Hill offers a network of hiking trails that will take you around its perimeter or up to its summit. The place gets crowded on July 4, when Tubbs offers prime viewing for the fireworks show. Other times of the year, celebrate the end of your hike with a Gooey, the signature ice cream sundae at the Dockside restaurant at the Coeur d'Alene Resort. These large sundaes are meant for sharing. The Chocolate Obsession features white chocolate ice cream, chocolate mousse, brownie bites, chocolate chunks, and hot fudge, while the signature Butterfinger Hot Fudge Gooey includes Butterfinger candy bars, chocolate and vanilla ice cream, hot fudge, chocolate swirls, and whipped cream. Grab a spoon!

Tubbs Hill: Downtown Coeur d'Alene, with trailheads on 10th Street
and near the Third Street boat ramp, next to the resort.
cdaid.org/763/departments/parks/all-parks/tubbs-hill

Coeur d'Alene Resort: 115 S. 2nd St., Coeur d'Alene, 855-703-4648
cdaresort.com

HIT THE TRAIL
BELOW HIGH DRIVE

Unique among city parks is the swath of 500 acres, mostly ponderosa pine forest, sloping down from High Drive to Hangman Creek. Most of the South Hill bluff's twenty-three miles of trails were built on the sly by enthusiasts who had a vision if not an official plan. Other hikers, runners, mountain bikers, and nature lovers have followed through the haunts of coyotes, moose, deer, and other critters. The trails are unmarked. Starting from High Drive and 37th or 29th avenues, head down from the sidewalk a few steps to the first trail paralleling the bluff rim and explore. Some trails lead down to overlooks of Hangman Creek (also known as Latah Creek) and offer a good workout climbing back up. April to May features a booming bloom of golden arrowleaf balsamroot.

509-625-6200
friendsofthebluff.org

RAFT DEVIL'S TOENAIL

You're not truly in touch with the Spokane River until your face has been slapped to attention by a frothing whitewater wave. The river's most exciting float runs from T. J. Meenach Bridge to Plese Flats in Riverside State Park. If you choose to brave this two-hour voyage, be ready to navigate tricky and potentially lethal hydraulics through the Bowl and Pitcher. After regaining composure with a breather in easy water, you'll be angling for the perfect line to plunge past a prominent spire of rock emerging from a rapid known as Devil's Toenail. This is not a run for tubers or novice boaters. Even some experienced paddlers have found religion at the foot of the Devil. Several rafting companies provide guides and gear to make this bucket-list adventure available and safe even to landlubbers.

1701 W. Water Ave.
888-502-1900; 509-998-1120
riverrafting.net

TIP
Spring (wet or dry suits required) through early July is prime time before the river drops too low to avoid rocks in the rapids.

SNAP A SELFIE WITH A TRUMPETER SWAN
AT TURNBULL NATIONAL WILDLIFE REFUGE

Here's a nature experience to toot your horn about: Drum up the patience to sit by a pond in Turnbull National Wildlife Refuge until a rare trumpeter swan feels comfortable enough to swim within selfie range. Trumpeters, the largest waterfowl species native to North America, were nearly extinct by the late 1950s before seed groups of the swans were brought to several refuges in the 1960s. The majestic white birds with the clarion call took hold at Turnbull. Although numbers dwindled to a single male at the refuge for a couple of decades, one or two pairs a year have been nesting on small impoundments near refuge headquarters. The entry fee is $3 a vehicle. The wildlife viewing potential for waterfowl and a range of critters is priceless.

26010 S. Smith Road, Cheney
509-235-4723
fws.gov/turnbull

BIKE WITH THE HUMAN-POWERED MASS

There's a moment on every bike ride. Your legs are tired, your bum is sore, and that next hill—forget it. But when you're surrounded by hundreds of other riders, you have no choice. Peer pressure and your competitive spirit ensures that your legs will pump and that hill will be conquered. And when you're riding between 9 and 116 miles, the vistas on two marquee Spokane-area rides definitely help distract the mind from the pain. Do you want a view of the majestic Lake Coeur d'Alene? Ride the Coeur d'Fondo. Or do you prefer the slow ramble of the Spokane River? Do Spokefest. Either way, you win. Your bum? Maybe not so much.

The Coeur d'Fondo offers five rides between 15 and 116 miles.
cdagranfondo.com

Spokefest has three rides, from nine to fifty miles.
spokefest.org

TIP
Bring snacks, water, and chamois cream.

STAND ON MOUNT SPOKANE'S SUMMIT

This is a quest for all seasons. You can reach the top of the highest peak in the area by hiking, biking, horse riding, and driving in summer and by snowshoeing, skiing, snowmobiling, or chairlift in winter. The view is astounding, including a bird's-eye view of the area's lakes. The paved Summit Road, open from early June into October, is the easiest course through 13,919-acre Mount Spokane State Park to Vista House at the top. Although shorter summit hikes are available from trailheads farther up the mountain, serious hikers should go for the max with a thigh-burning base-to-summit hike, about five miles one way, or ten miles round trip if you don't stash a bike or shuttle vehicle at the top. Vehicles in the park during summer must display a Washington Discover Pass (discoverpass.wa.gov.)

26107 N. Mount Spokane Park Dr., Mead
509-238-4258
mountspokane.org

HIKE TO A HIDDEN WATERFALL
AT INDIAN CANYON PARK

Mystic Falls tumbles over a basalt cliff into a deep ravine, creating a small grotto in Indian Canyon Park. It's a charming spot, but you have to clamber down a steep trail to view the falls. It's worth the trek. Once you park in the trailhead lot, walk to the short loop trail and follow the sound of rushing water to the top of the falls. Shrubs screen the view into the ravine, but you'll find a few side trails that take you down to the base of the waterfall. In the spring, yellow and green lichen paint the nearby rocks. Lush vegetation around the waterfall is reminiscent of the Washington Cascades. Chief Spokane Garry spent the final years of his life at a nearby camp in Indian Canyon. The ravine is full of birdsong, but since this is West Spokane, you'll also hear overhead jets approaching Spokane International Airport.

Info: Trailhead parking lot is at 4812 W. Canyon Drive.

TIP
Bring bug spray. Mosquitoes are thick here.

SHOOT CLAYS
AT THE SPOKANE GUN CLUB

No sport in the area has deeper roots than shooting competition, and few clubs can boast a longer-running tenure than the Spokane Gun Club. Founded in 1892, the park-like spread of trap and skeet ranges is in Spokane Valley, where members still welcome newbies to take a shot. Organized shooting was enormously popular in the 1800s, with the largest events held on Thanksgiving, Christmas, and New Year. Except for the voice-operated traps, not a lot has changed about the sport in the past century. The trick is to stand sixteen yards from the traphouse, shoulder a shotgun, call "Pull," and then try to lead and smoke a 4 5/16-inch round clay target that's speeding away on a random angle at sixty feet per second. It's easier than it looks, sometimes.

19615 E. Sprague Ave., Spokane Valley
509-926-6505
spokanegunclub.com

TIP
Club members don't care whether you're a hot shot or not, but they have no tolerance for sloppy gun handling. Safety is paramount.

MOUNTAIN BIKE
AT BEACON HILL

Craving the adrenaline rush of skiing? The mental challenge of picking the perfect line and riding it to its conclusion? But there isn't any snow? Beacon Hill has got you covered. Just twenty minutes from downtown Spokane, this popular single-track mountain bike course offers everything a dirt shredder could want. There are jumps, technical descents, and a brand-spanking-new pump track. But what makes Beacon Hill stand out is its proximity to downtown and the wide range of options. With more than thirty trails crisscrossing about 1,000 acres, there is something for everyone.

TIP

Take a class. Evergreen East, Spokane's mountain biking group, offers mountain biking classes. Visit evergreeneast.org.

FLY DOWN
THE ROCK WATER SLIDES
NEAR PRIEST LAKE

Slip. Slip. Slide. These natural water slides near Idaho's Priest Lake will give you the joy of a traditional waterslide with none of the fees or lines. Getting there takes some effort. The slides are about eighty miles from Spokane, and then about a mile and a half hike from the trailhead. But it's well worth it. Water slickened rock makes for a fun, fast descent. Bring a plastic bag to sit on and, if you're wanting some extra luxury, foam to pad your seat.

Info: Drive to Lionhead Campground (314 Indian Creek Park Road, Coolin, Idaho). But instead of turning left into Lionhead, turn right onto a gravel road and follow it for five miles.

SEE SNOWY OWLS
IN THE WILD

Every winter a cast of winged characters fit for a Harry Potter movie sweeps onto the open fields of Eastern Washington. With a bit of luck and patience, you might see some of the snowy owls that leave the deep snows of Canada and fly south. Unlike their nocturnal relatives, snowy owls are active during the day, often perched on fence posts, old farm machinery, buildings, and power poles. Good binoculars, a thermos of hot chocolate, and a map showing country roads are helpful for this chilly pursuit. Some of the hotspots in years past have been near Reardan. Some people swear by the cemetery in Davenport.

TIP
Go online to check for recent sightings, including *The Spokesman-Review*'s Outdoors reports, the local Audubon Society chapter, and other bird-watching groups.

PICK HUCKLEBERRIES
IN MOUNT SPOKANE STATE PARK

While people brag up their "secret" picking locations, the tangy-tart purple berries aren't hard to find. Huckleberry bushes abound at Mount Spokane State Park and on national forest lands. The shrubs grow at elevations of 4,000 feet and higher. Huckleberry season runs from mid- to late summer. Commercial harvest of huckleberries is forbidden, but in the Colville National Forest, you are allowed to pick three gallons of huckleberries. On the Idaho Panhandle National Forest, you can harvest a "reasonable amount" for personal use. Filling a gallon bucket requires patience. Huckleberries aren't abundant, but the flavor makes them worth the effort. So pack a lunch, water, and bear spray for a summer outing. You'll save about $45 to $60, which is the going rate for a gallon of fresh huckleberries at the farmers market.

Colville National Forest
fs.usda.gov/colville

Idaho Panhandle National Forest
fs.usda.gov/ipnf

Mount Spokane State Park
parks.state.wa.us/549/Mount-Spokane

TIP

Yes, bear spray is a necessity. Bears love huckleberries, too. And be careful not to damage the shrub while you're picking. Cutting down bushes can garner Forest Service fines starting at $250.

Photo credit: Colin Mulvany

CULTURE AND HISTORY

VISIT
THE LIBRARY WITH A VIEW

They call it The Lens—the upper floor of the Spokane Public Library downtown—and it's among the best views of the Spokane River flowing through the center of the city. Part of the library's effort to expand its programming beyond its ample book-lending system, The Lens is a third-floor stage and event space that hosts musical acts, readings, and *Lilac City Live*, a local talk show. The downtown library, the center of the citywide system, also has the Northwest Room, featuring important historical documents, a collection of genealogical resources, and a co-working space. Prepare to be distracted from what you're reading if you sit anywhere near the wall of windows on either floor.

906 W. Main Ave.
509-444-5300
spokanelibrary.org/downtown

FEED
THE GARBAGE GOAT

Why are there so many conscientious kids in Riverfront Park picking up cigarette butts and discarded napkins? Because picking up trash has never been so fun. Spokane's Garbage Goat, a steel sculpture whose mouth doubles as a trash vacuum, has an unassuming presence in Riverfront Park. The goat sits off to the side, not far from the Looff Carrousel. Kids find it and can't stop feeding him. When the trash is gone, they look for leaves and mulch so they can keep pressing the vacuum button. The attraction is the creation of Spokane sculptor Sister Paula Turnbull, who made the anti-litter attraction for Spokane's Expo '74, the first world's fair with an environmental theme.

507 N. Howard St.
509-625-6600

DRINK IN WORDS, WINE, AND LIVE MUSIC
AT NORTHWEST PASSAGES

Listen to and mingle with nationally known and bestselling authors, storytellers, innovators, and newsmakers. Enjoy a glass of cabernet franc at the elegant and airy Terra Blanca Wine Bar. Take a newsroom tour and witness firsthand how a community newspaper comes together each day. If all this sounds good, then a night at Northwest Passages Book Club and Community Forum is a must when you're in Spokane. The family-owned *Spokesman-Review* now opens the doors of its historic downtown building for forums featuring lively on-stage conversations that draw audience members into the discussion. And Northwest Passages is a bargain: General admission typically is $5 or free, chocolate chip cookies included.

999 W. Riverside Ave.
509-459-5403
Spokesman.com/bookclub

TIP

Spokesman-Review editor Rob Curley offers guided tours, filled with lots of history and laughs, up to the newspaper's clock tower and grinning gargoyles. Message bookclub@ spokesman.com to find out how to book one.

GET SMART
AT GET LIT!

It's Hoopfest for book lovers. For a week every April, the city welcomes some of the best writers in the country—and the city—for the annual literary festival sponsored by Eastern Washington University. For twenty years, Get Lit! has brought in big-name writers, such as Joyce Carol Oates, Kurt Vonnegut, Anne Lamott, Colson Whitehead, and many others, while also providing events for regional writers and readers of all ages, including thousands of local students. The Pie & Whiskey readings are always popular. Get in line early.

getlitfestival.org/

TIP
Check out a slam poetry event; Spokane's become one of the strongest slam cities in the country.

EAT AN ELEPHANT EAR
AT THE FAIR

Its official name is the Spokane County Interstate Fair. And it's held every year in September for ten days, beginning on the Friday after Labor Day. But no one calls it that. It's just called The Fair. It has all of the things you'd expect at a large regional fair—brightly colored carnival rides and games, llamas at the petting zoo, tons of vendors (including more hot tub sellers than you can imagine), thousands of exhibits, and—of course—pig races. Those are all great, but if you want to really experience Spokane's fair, then you order an elephant ear. Don't worry, it's not really an elephant's ear. It's oddly shaped fried flat dough, covered in sugar and cinnamon . . . and roughly the size of an elephant's ear. You can add other toppings, but the only one that matters is huckleberries. Go wait in the longest line and see why the fair's most popular elephant ear stand uses 30 pounds of cinnamon and 1,200 pounds of sugar every summer.

Spokane County Fair & Expo Center, 404 N. Havana St.
509-477-1766
spokanecounty.org/982/Fair-Expo-Center

SPEND AN AFTERNOON
AT THE MAC

Spokane, perhaps unfairly, isn't known for its art and culture scene. The Northwest Museum of Arts and Culture (MAC) is one reason that should change. The MAC has been a cultural landmark since its founding in 1916. Set in the historic Browne's Addition neighborhood, the museum features a rotating cast of exhibitions in a variety of media. A recent visit featured an exhibit on modern origami, the process of cataloguing artifacts, paintings of Spokane circa 1912, and a local sculptor's collection. The MAC encourages you to explore and create, tucking art into every corner of the building and having spaces specifically for patrons to color or draw. While it might not get the notoriety of some of the area's other attractions, an afternoon at the MAC is well worth your time.

2316 W. First Ave.
509-456-3931
northwestmuseum.org

TIP
Go early and check out the Campbell House next door for a look at how the wealthy lived in the early 1900s.

HONOR AN AMERICAN HERO
ON A SCULPTURE WALKING TOUR

On a low pedestal in the breezeway behind the INB Performing Arts Center kneels a bronze figure wearing the spacesuit of a NASA astronaut. The statue honors Michael Phillip Anderson, whose quiet curiosity, deep conviction, and love of science carried him from Cheney to the very limits of humanity's reach. Anderson served aboard the *Columbia* space shuttle, conducting experiments from Earth's orbit. On Feb. 1, 2003, the shuttle broke apart and disintegrated, killing all on board. Anderson's memory lives on here, and you can visit the statue as part of a self-guided Sculpture Walk of public art. Compiled by the Spokane Parks Department, the downtown tour also features other iconic works in Riverfront Park, including *Centennial Sculpture* by the late Harold Balasz and David Govedare's *The Joy of Running Together*.

Info: The Anderson statute is directly behind the INB Performing Arts Center, 334 W. Spokane Falls Blvd.

The Sculpture Walk map is here: my.spokanecity.org/riverfrontpark/highlights/sculpture-walk/

GAWK AT FINE OLD BUILDINGS
AT THE HEART OF THE CITY

One of the first things you'll notice about downtown Spokane: The streets are lined with graceful, hundred-year-old buildings. You'll want to hit the streets to explore and admire the historic structures that span the heart of the city, stretching east from Monroe Street to Washington Street and north from First Avenue to Spokane Falls Boulevard. Many are built of brick or stone, sometimes adorned with terra cotta tile, and represent several styles and Spokane's earliest architectural stars. Be sure to stroll by the intersection of Riverside Avenue and Stevens Street. The Fernwell Building, a Romanesque Revival classic, occupies the southwest corner. It's just one of many architectural gems.

TIP

It's best to go on foot because the largest buildings look their best from the opposite side of the street. Visit Spokane (visitspokane.com) and the Spokane City/County Historic Preservation Office (historicspokane.org) include annotated maps on their websites. Contact groupcoordinators.com for guided tours.

VISIT
THE BING CROSBY HOUSE AND MUSEUM

The biggest Hollywood star ever to rise from Spokane still shines bright in a small museum at the edge of the Gonzaga University campus. The Bing Crosby House Museum, which occupies the first floor of the 1911 home where the velvet-voiced crooner grew up, celebrates the life and career of an entertainment colossus through photos, keepsakes, and memorabilia dating from Bing's boyhood to his 1977 death on a golf course in Spain. Unless you're of a certain age, it might be hard to grasp just how big Bing really was. Consider this: Bing ruled the recording industry, movies, television, and radio for the better part of three decades. He had more hit songs than Elvis, the Beatles, and Michael Jackson combined. Museum admission is free.

508 E. Sharp Ave.
509-313-3847
researchguides.gonzaga.edu/bingcrosbyhouse

REVEL
IN LILAC CITY

Every May, Spokane celebrates its status as the Lilac City. There are several ways to join the celebration, including a visit to the quiet of the Lilac Garden in Manito Park, where lilac bushes were first planted in 1912. (Spokane has its own hybrid, a double-blooming fragrant beauty called Syringa that changes from mauve to pink, then silver, and finally apple-blossom white.) You'll also want to join the pomp and wonder of the Lilac Festival Armed Forces Torchlight Parade. The streets of downtown are transformed into a marching band bonanza, as more than three dozen high schools send student musicians to the parade. People line the curbs to enjoy the floats, horses, marching bands, classic cars, and, of course, the military members and veterans passing by.

Manito Park: 1702 S. Grand Blvd.
my.spokanecity.org/parks/gardens/lilac

Lilac Festival Armed Forces Torchlight Parade:
spokanelilacfestival.org/parade

TIP
The parade is popular. Arrive early, like three hours early, to get a curbside spot for your lawn chairs.

GO TO A POWWOW

Three area tribes—the Coeur d'Alene, Spokane, and the Kalispel—hold summer powwows, and each offers attendees a unique chance to experience Native American culture and traditions. The Coeur d'Alene tribe holds Julyamsh, which features a horse parade, drum circle, and other activities at the Kootenai County Fairgrounds. The Spokane Tribe of Indians hosts the Gathering at the Falls, which brings singers and dancers of all ages to Riverfront Park. At the Kalispel Reservation, the annual powwow includes a buffalo barbecue, stick games, and a fun run. Be sure to ask before filming or taking photos at the celebrations.

Julyamsh
julyamsh.com/

Kalispel Powwow
kalispeltribe.com/calendar/event/4067/

Gathering at the Falls
gatfpowwow.org

CATCH A ROMANTIC SCENE
ATOP CLIFF DRIVE

Stand on the basalt bluff of Cliff Drive and enjoy a fantastic panoramic view of Spokane. The best time to go is at dusk, just as the city lights come alive. From this vantage point, downtown Spokane is the prominent feature, but you also can see a sweeping view of the entire city. It's a favorite spot of professional and amateur photographers alike. With a dark sky to the north and evening light on the buildings, the results are spectacular. Also, check out Cliff Park, at 13th Avenue and Grove Street, just two blocks to the south, where you can climb the steep steps up the top of its large outcropping. With few visitors, the grassy top is a great place to have a romantic picnic.

TIP
Parking is not allowed on Cliff Drive, but you can park on South Stevens Street, which is right across from the public viewpoint.

TAKE A MANSION WALKING TOUR
OF BROWNE'S ADDITION

If you enjoy seeing historic homes of the rich and famous, take a walk through Browne's Addition, the city's earliest upscale residential district. Barely a mile west of downtown, the self-contained neighborhood includes a stock of century-old mansions built for pioneer business leaders and their families. Scattered apartment buildings, some of them equally historic, dot the area. The 2300 block of West First Avenue, including the Northwest Museum of Arts and Culture, has nine residential classics, three of them designed by famed local architect Kirtland Cutter. Be sure to see Cutter's extravagant Patsy Clark mansion, facing Coeur d'Alene Park, at Second Avenue and Hemlock Street. (The museum sells a detailed map.)

Info: Arrange guided tours at groupcoordinators.com.

TIP

To see more fine old homes and mansions, follow the right-hand fork uphill on South Stevens Street and turn right onto Sumner Avenue. The left fork turns east past Providence Sacred Heart Medical Center and onto Rockwood Boulevard, the centerpiece of a National Register Historic District.

SOAK UP PALISADES PARK

There's no shortage of natural beauty and outdoor recreational opportunities in the Spokane area, but on a clear day, with Mount Spokane standing stark against the skyline, you won't find better views of the city and its natural features than from Palisades Park. Comprising 700 acres of conservation and city park land, with varying, well-maintained trail loops for hikers, bikers, and horses, the park's proximity to the city and ease of access make it a popular spot on any day of the week when the weather is fine. The basalt cliffs for which the park is named offer striking examples of the region's geology, and a natural creek and waterfall add to the scenic beauty.

Info: located west of the city near Indian Canyon Golf Course,
at the junction of Greenwood Road, Rimrock Drive, and Basalt Road.
palisadesnw.com

DRIVE TO THE TOP
OF STEPTOE BUTTE

Rising above the rumpled landscape of the Palouse is a mass of quartzite older than most other rock in the Pacific Northwest. Steptoe Butte State Park is about fifty-five miles south of Spokane, an hour's drive through small towns and some of the world's richest farm fields from which bountiful wheat harvests are shipped across the globe. It's the perfect place to witness the legendary beauty of the Palouse and to learn a little something about the region's natural history. Awe-inspiring views atop 3,612-foot Steptoe Butte might also include hawks, vultures, and perhaps a hang glider. Bring a picnic lunch to enjoy at this day-use destination beneath an oasis of shade trees.

Steptoe Butte State Park, Whitman County
509-337-6457
parks.state.wa.us/592/Steptoe-Butte

TIP
Washington State Parks require a Discover Pass. A day pass is $11.50, or $35 for a year. Buy them at store.discoverpass.wa.gov/ or where hunting and fishing licenses are sold.

TAKE A PORTRAIT
AT FINCH ARBORETUM

If you've chosen Spokane for your family reunion (or wedding or prom or work picnic), you'll find no better place to get your group portrait than at Finch Arboretum, which covers sixty-five acres of wooded hills. Not far from the parking lot is a white willow that may be the most photographed tree in the Inland Northwest. The tree has branches that rival the size of impressive trunks. One in particular is nearly parallel to the ground and low enough to climb. The result, if done right, is a picture reminiscent of the famous Depression-era shot, *Lunch Atop a Skyscraper*. The tree was planted in the late 1940s when military housing was on the land. A resident, May (Jinotti) Sharp, planted it from a sapling from her grandmother's yard in Idaho.

3404 W. Woodland Blvd.
509-624-4832
my.spokanecity.org/urbanforestry/programs/finch-arboretum

TIP
There's much more to see at Finch, including 2,000 species, a trail for the blind, and Garden Springs Creek, which is being restored to a more natural state in hopes that trout may repopulate it.

SEE WHERE THEY MADE THE MOVIE

Several popular films have been shot in and around Spokane, and you can visit many of the locations. Head to the Garland District to see the iconic Milk Bottle, which was featured in an exterior shot in the Johnny Depp film *Benny & Joon*. Ferguson's Cafe next door was heavily damaged by fire in 2011 (and the Milk Bottle also was damaged) after serving as a location in *Benny & Joon*, *Vision Quest*, and *Why Would I Lie*. *Vision Quest* star Matthew Modine appeared at a special screening of his coming-of-age drama in 2012 to raise funds for the café's reconstruction. Speaking of *Vision Quest*, the 1985 film marked the screen debut of Madonna, whose scenes were set at the Bigfoot Tavern on Spokane's North Side.

Ferguson's Cafe/Mary Lou's Milk Bottle
804 and 802 W. Garland Ave.

The Bigfoot Tavern
9115 N. Division St.

CHECK OUT A CHIHULY
AT THE JUNDT ART MUSEUM

On the western edge of Gonzaga University's campus is the home of the Gonzaga Red Chandelier, the only work by glass sculptor Dale Chihuly on permanent public display in Spokane. It hangs from the ceiling in a circular room in the Jundt Art Museum that overlooks a sculpture garden and the Spokane River. The museum's permanent collection includes more than 5,000 pieces, ranging from works by old masters such as Rembrandt and Goya to modernists including Picasso and Warhol. Admission is free.

502 E. Boone Ave.
509-313-6843
gonzaga.edu/student-life/arts-culture/jundt-art-museum

TIP

No art tour of the Inland Northwest is complete without a trip sixty miles south to Pullman to see the Jordan Schnitzer Museum of Art at Washington State University. Opened in 2018 in the new Crimson Cube, the museum holds an extensive collection of prints by acclaimed artist Jim Dine, who now lives in Walla Walla, and prints and photographs by Andy Warhol, as well as art glass and paintings from the Safeco Collection. museum.wsu.edu

SHOPPING AND FASHION

GET LOST
AT AUNTIE'S

Auntie's is the center of Spokane's literary world, the city's oldest independent bookstore, the home of countless readings by local and visiting authors, and an easy best place to lose an hour browsing in the stacks. Auntie's opened in 1978, and the bookstore has been in its current location in the Liberty Building downtown since 1994. Auntie's carries a large selection of new and used books, cards, T-shirts, and gifts. It also has a section dedicated to the latest books by local authors.

402 W. Main Ave.
509-838-0206
auntiesbooks.com

TIP
Another excellent indie is the Well-Read Moose in Coeur d'Alene. This small space in the Riverstone development has a well-curated selection of local favorites and national best sellers, along with a café that serves sandwiches and pastry, as well as coffee, beer, and wine.

GET YOUR MOCKINGBIRD FIX
AT ATTICUS AND BOO RADLEY'S

Two eclectic gift shops with names inspired by the classic novel *To Kill a Mockingbird* are musts for downtown browsers. Boo Radley's offers a diverse range of the offbeat, unexpected, and interesting—from some of the best snarky local T-shirts to gag gifts to vintage toys to Funko Pops. Just up the street at Atticus, you'll find coffee in every form, as well as a selection of gifts for the home, teas, stationery, and other items. In the back of the store is one of downtown's best coffee shops and meeting places, which also serves simple, delicious sandwiches and other treats.

Boo Radley's
232 N. Howard St.
509-456-7479

Atticus
222 N. Howard St.
509-747-0336

TIP
At Atticus, check out the cool Vintage Spokane art prints by Chris Bovey and pieces inspired by the late Spokane artist Harold Balazs.

FIND HIDDEN GEMS AND ANTIQUES

Looking for popular mid-century modern pieces? Vintage twists for décor? Make it easy with quick stops at two Spokane antiquing hotspots: North Monroe's shopping district and nearby Hillyard. Stop along Market Street to find United Hillyard Antique Mall, two stories stocked full of treasures, along with other nearby shops. Along Monroe, you can park and walk among shops, like the store Metro Eclectic featuring mid-century furnishings and nearby Antique Gallery stocking a gamut of true antiques. Or head to Northwest Boulevard for an eclectic mix at Boulevard Mercantile, from lighted airplane décor that once flew over an Airway Heights hotel to record-cabinet rehabs with new turntables and bluetooth units. Other treasure hunts can range from Tossed and Found to Ross's Memories on Monroe.

United Hillyard Antique Mall
5016 N. Market St.
509-483-2647
hillyardantiquemall.com

Metro Eclectic
604 N. Monroe St.
509-325-5400
metroeclectic.com

Antique Gallery
620 N. Monroe St.
509-325-3864

Boulevard Mercantile
1905 N. Monroe St.
509-327-7547

Tossed and Found
2607 N. Monroe St.
509-325-2607

Ross's Memories on Monroe
2606 N. Monroe St.
509-991-2513

HUNT FOR TREASURES
AT FARM CHICKS

It started in 2002 with a barn sale of vintage and handmade goods. Now it's the Farm Chicks Vintage and Handmade Fair, a show and sale that draws hundreds of curated vendors and thousands of shoppers to the Spokane County Fair & Expo Center the first full weekend of June each year. Check out vintage fabrics, art, antiques, jewelry, handcrafted goods, rehabbed furniture, and vintage home decor: Chances are good that if you're looking for it, you'll find it.

Spokane County Fair and Expo Center
404 N. Havana St., Spokane Valley
thefarmchicks.com

HANG OUT
AT MERLYN'S COMIC BOOK SHOP

Merlyn's is what a comic book shop should look and feel like: Old building, wooden floors, boxes upon boxes upon boxes of comics, and a knowledgeable staff. The downtown store also has an exceptional collection of role-playing games and card games such as Magic. While the kids (and their dads) are thumbing through comics, others can slip next door for a bit of shopping, eating, and drinking at the open market that is Saranac Commons. For those with a sweet tooth, the miniature pecan pies at Common Crumb beckon.

15 W. Main Ave.
509-624-0957
merlyns.biz

INDULGE
IN A SPA DAY

De-stress with a treatment at one of Spokane's spas. Most offer a full range of exfoliation treatments, mud wraps, facials, waxing, manicures, pedicures, and massages in settings that will leave you feeling relaxed and rejuvenated. At the Historic Davenport Hotel, you can make an overnight experience of it. The spa, tucked into the lower level of the gilded downtown hotel, features overnight spa packages for couples as well as individuals. The top-rated La Rive Spa at the Northern Quest Resort and Casino in Airway Heights also offers overnight spa packages. Amenities include experiential showers, an indoor pool and whirlpool, and cedar warming rooms. Services at La Rive all come with a glass of bubbly or Washington wine. Spa Paradiso, in Kendall Yards, overlooking the Centennial Trail and Spokane River, is a day spa where guests can book full day, half day, or single-service treatments. Look online for last-minute deals.

Spa and Salon at the Historic Davenport Hotel
10 S. Post St.
509-789-7300
davenporthotelcollection.com

**La Rive Spa at the Northern Quest
Resort and Casino**
100 N. Hayford Rd., Airway Heights
509-481-6108
northernquest.com

Spa Paradiso
1237 W. Summit Parkway, Suite A
509-747-3529
spaparadiso.com

SHOP
LOCAL ARTISANS

Anyone can find their way to the mall (the Spokane area has three). But when you travel to a new city, it can be a challenge to find just the right locally made goodies for yourself or loved ones at home. The Pop Up Shop in the Steam Plant Square offers pottery, jewelry, body care, leather goods, and the popular "Spokane Doesn't Suck" T-shirt, with proceeds supporting local artists and arts programs. For ceramics, check out Pottery Place Plus, nestled in the same building as Auntie's Bookstore, for mugs, bowls, and other items made by regional potters. At local candymaker Halletts, grab a bite of Huckleberry Bliss. At River Park Square, pop into Made in Washington for smoked salmon, jam, and other regional treats.

Pop Up Shop
159 S. Lincoln St.
terrainspokane.com/popupshop

Pottery Place Plus
203 N. Washington St.
509-327-6920
potteryplaceplus.com

Halletts
6704 N. Nevada St. No. 1
509-474-0899
hallettschocolates.com

Made in Washington
808 W. Main Ave., No. 223
509-838-1517
originalmadeinwa.com

SHOP ON A BUDGET

Save money in stylish bliss. Several Spokane stores sell upscale brands of apparel items, subtly second-hand or never worn, at much lower prices. Think of them as classy rethreads. The region's thrift stores have hidden treasures, too, often well-sorted by style and colors at places like Goodwill or Value Village. At shops like Fringe & Fray, the Reclothery, or Echo Boutique, you'll find an array of wardrobe choices and accessories neatly arranged in cozy settings. Teens can find fashionable trends at two locations of Plato's Closet. Need fancy attire for that special occasion? Chances are you'll find a never-worn dress with an original tag of $99, down to $49. Other dresses, such as those at Echo Boutique, range from $18 to $30. Fringe & Fray carries trendy men's clothing, too.

Fringe & Fray
1325 W. First Ave.
509-720-7116
fringeandfray.net

The Reclothery
613 S. Washington St.
509-624-9741
thereclothery.com

Echo Boutique
1033 W. First Ave.
509-747-0890
echoboutiquespokane.com

Plato's Closet
5628 N. Division St.
509-484-3700
15735 E. Broadway Ave., Spokane Valley
509-924-5600
platosclosetspokane.com

SUGGESTED
ITINERARIES

FAMILY FUN

Take a Spin on the Looff Carrousel, 56

Slide Down the Big Red Wagon, 57

Play Catch on the Field at an Indians Game, 62

Pick Your Own at Green Bluff, 16

Eat an Elephant Ear at the Fair, 97

Eat Breakfast on a Train at Frank's Diner, 2

Watch the Planes over Breakfast at Felts Field, 12

Find a Swimming Hole, 71

Pitch in at a River Clean-up, 61

OUTDOORS

Join the Dawn Patrol at Mount Spokane, 64

Zip Across Mica Peak, 63

Stand on Mount Spokane's Summit, 81

Thrill to a Fantastic SkyRide, 52

Tube the Spokane River, 54

Take a Bald Eagle Tour at Lake Coeur d'Alene, 72

SPORTS

CUISINE

CULTURE

• •

ACTIVITIES
BY SEASON

SPRING

Get Smart at Get Lit!, 96

Run Bloomsday, 60

Revel in Lilac City, 103

SUMMER

Hit the Streets for Hoopfest, 59

Hunt for Treasures at Farm Chicks, 120

Pig Out in the Park, 35

Party for a Cause at Gleason Fest, 49

Get a Scoop at the Scoop, 14

Paddle to No-Li Brewhouse, 15

Tube the Spokane River, 54

Paint the Town at Summer Art Festivals, 38

FALL

Eat an Elephant Ear at the Fair, 97

Follow the Ale Trail, 27

Pick Your Own at Green Bluff, 16

Take a Bald Eagle Tour at Lake Coeur d'Alene, 72

WINTER

Skate the Ice Ribbon, 58

Ring in the New Year for the Symphony, 48

Join the Dawn Patrol at Mount Spokane, 64

• •

Photo credit: Jesse Tinsley

INDEX

Photo credit: Tyler Tjomsland